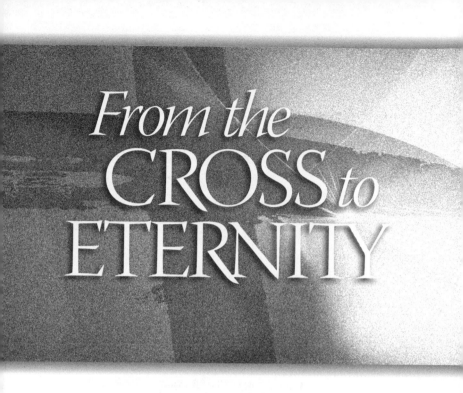

From the
CROSS *to*
ETERNITY

*Seven Words That Will
Change Your Life Forever*

Randal Ross

THE
ACCESS
GROUP

CONTENTS

THEN JESUS SAID, *"Father, forgive them,*
for they do not know what they do."
AND THEY DIVIDED HIS GARMENTS AND CAST LOTS.

AND JESUS SAID TO HIM, *"Assuredly, I say to you,*
today you will be with Me in Paradise."

WHEN JESUS THEREFORE SAW HIS MOTHER,
AND THE DISCIPLE WHOM HE LOVED STANDING BY,
HE SAID TO HIS MOTHER, *"Woman, behold your son!"*

AND ABOUT THE NINTH HOUR JESUS CRIED OUT
WITH A LOUD VOICE, SAYING, *"Eli, Eli, lama sabachthani?"*
THAT IS, *"My God, My God, why have You forsaken Me?"*

AFTER THIS, JESUS, KNOWING THAT ALL THINGS
WERE NOW ACCOMPLISHED, THAT THE SCRIPTURE
MIGHT BE FULFILLED, SAID, *"I thirst!"*

SO WHEN JESUS HAD RECEIVED THE SOUR WINE,
HE SAID, *"It is finished!"*
AND BOWING HIS HEAD, HE GAVE UP HIS SPIRIT.

AND WHEN JESUS HAD CRIED OUT WITH A LOUD VOICE,
HE SAID, *"Father, 'into Your hands I commit My spirit.'"*
HAVING SAID THIS, HE BREATHED HIS LAST.

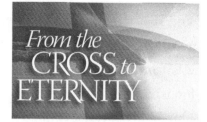

From the
CROSS *to*
ETERNITY

THE GREATEST DAY

If you had to name the most important event in history, what would you choose? Some people might think of a crucial battle or a great scientific break-through. But those who have an understanding of God's plan for this world would agree that the great-est event in history took place the day Jesus Christ died on the cross for our sins.

The Incarnation, the Cross, and the Resurrection are all tied together. None of them stands alone, and each of them is essential for our salvation. In the Incarnation, God becomes man. On the cross, God dies for mankind. With the Resurrection, God over-comes death and hell. But of the three, the cross of Jesus stands at the epicenter of God's plan of redemption and restoration. The Bible emphasizes this fact numerous times.

Consider 1 Corinthians 1:18: "For the message of the cross is foolishness to those who are perishing, but to us who are being saved it is the power of God."

Or Galatians 6:14, 15: "But God forbid that I should boast except in the cross of our Lord Jesus Christ, by whom the world has been crucified to me, and I to the world. For in Christ Jesus neither circumcision nor uncircumcision avails anything, but a new creation."

Or Colossians 1:19-22: "For it pleased the Father that in Him all the fullness should dwell, and by Him to reconcile all things to Himself, by Him, whether things on earth or things in heaven, having made peace through the blood of His cross. And you, who once were alienated and enemies in your mind by wicked works, yet now He has reconciled in the body of His flesh through death, to present you holy, and blameless, and above reproach in His sight."

I am convinced that spiritual confidence, emotional strength, and supernatural power come from knowing what Christ accomplished on the cross.

My hope is that as you read the following pages you will understand our great salvation better and learn to apply it, not only with an eternal perspective, but also as you live out its message daily.

This book examines the last, the shortest, the hardest, and perhaps the most powerful sermon Jesus ever preached. In just seven short statements from the cross, He expounded on some of the deepest truths of this life and the next.

When life is hard, every word matters. Every word from the cross was spoken with purpose and life-changing power. Not a syllable was wasted. His last words teach us how to gain victory in times when we are hurting, alone or attacked by evil.

The question that led me to study Christ's words from the cross rests squarely with our reason for being as His followers: How can we win this generation to Christ? We live in a skeptical, jaded, and mistrusting world. How can we overcome barriers and help people see that one ultimate truth—the truth of the crucifixion—will open eternity to them?

Most of us hardly know where to begin in communicating resurrection truth to people from a completely nonbiblical background. Yet these same people watch and listen when we go through the hard places. They take note of how we function under stress. On the cross, Jesus endured the most painful event in history—and He triumphed over it. His words on the cross become defining keys to that victory and to understanding who He is and what the gospel means.

The world came to the cross and watched. They listened to what Jesus said. What they heard became perhaps the most important words Jesus ever spoke. His short, direct, profound statements tell us who He is.

Through the power of the inspired record of the Crucifixion, every one of us has the privilege of standing at the cross with the crowd. Every one of us is equal, and every one of us has questions and even doubts.

And to us Jesus says, "Come and watch. Come and listen. Build your life on Me, and the storms will not wash you away. Take Me at My words. They work. They are life and light and victory."

I have included in the back of this book "Life's

Greatest Decision" by my friend and author Randy Hurst. If you have not yet made a decision to follow Christ, I pray that His last message from the cross will touch your heart and help you come to know His great love for you.

In the following pages, stand with me at the foot of the cross and hear the Savior speak. Watch and see that storms and problems are not greater than the power of God. Gain fresh insight into the life-giving truth that greater is He who is in you than he who is in the world.

Jesus' final words are important and sometimes challenging, but they lead us to the greater Resurrection experience. The cross and the tomb are not the end. God is leading us to what we need most—a mighty Resurrection breakthrough in our lives.

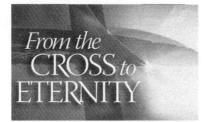

From the
CROSS *to*
ETERNITY

FATHER, FORGIVE THEM

"AND WHEN THEY HAD COME TO THE *place called Calvary, there they crucified Him, and the criminals, one on the right hand and the other on the left. Then Jesus said, "Father, forgive them, for they do not know what they do." And they divided His garments and cast lots. And the people stood looking on. But even the rulers with them sneered, saying, 'He saved others; let Him save Himself if He is the Christ, the chosen of God.' The soldiers also mocked Him, coming and offering Him sour wine, and saying, 'If You are the King of the Jews, save Yourself.' And an inscription also was written over Him in letters of Greek, Latin, and Hebrew: THIS IS THE KING OF THE JEWS"* (Luke 23:33-38).

This passage in Luke records what are thought to be Jesus' first words from the cross. Not surprisingly, He begins with forgiveness.

To see these words in context helps us understand how genuine forgiveness works. The setting was shortly after 9 o'clock on Passover morning. The city of Jerusalem was packed with worshipers, merchants, and tourists.

Just about everyone had turned against Jesus. He was betrayed by His friends, rejected by the priests who were chosen to serve in the temple, and sold out by the crowd who chose a murderer over Him when Pilate offered to free one criminal as a Passover gift.

Jesus was mocked by the Roman soldiers and then marched through the crowd, a hateful mob that added insult to His pain. Now the King of kings was hanging between two criminals—two men who would play a vital role in the story of salvation.

But the first words of Jesus weren't directed to those around Him; they were a prayer to His Father.

He didn't want God, the Righteous Judge, to punish His tormentors for what they were doing to Him. Jesus' first prayer on the cross was, "Father, forgive them." It is a startling prayer to hear from One so abused and cruelly treated. But it is so appropriate to everything Jesus will accomplish at Calvary, because the cross is ultimately about forgiveness. Without forgiveness nothing else matters.

FORGIVEN AND FORGIVING

Christians talk much about forgiveness because it is central to Jesus and His kingdom. Forgiveness is not just a good idea; it is essential in overcoming the attacks of the enemy. Receiving and giving forgiveness is vital to living in God's family. Jesus came to forgive our sins. He came to pay the penalty for sin by bringing us forgiveness through the cross.

The apostle Paul wrote, "And you, being dead in your trespasses and the uncircumcision of your flesh, He has made alive together with Him, having forgiven you all trespasses, having wiped out the handwriting of requirements that was against us, which was contrary to us. And He has taken it out of the way, having nailed it to the cross. Having disarmed principalities and powers, He made a public spectacle of them, triumphing over them in it" (Colossians 2:13-15).

Being a Christian means being forgiven, without condemnation for what we have done wrong. Because of the cross, we are forgiven completely. That is the good news of the cross. That is the reason Jesus was hanging there.

The Bible also teaches us not only to ask for forgiveness, but also to extend forgiveness to others. This is Christ's mark upon us. We see this central obligation of the believer expressed early on as Jesus taught on prayer. He told His disciples:

"In this manner, therefore, pray: Our Father in heaven, hallowed be Your name. Your kingdom come. Your will be done on earth as it is in heaven. Give us this day our daily bread. *And forgive us our debts, as we forgive our debtors.* And do not lead us into temptation, but deliver us from the evil one. For Yours is the kingdom and the power and the glory forever. Amen" (Matthew 6:9-13).

When the cross is effective in your life, you not only receive forgiveness. You also give it. And by forgiving people in Jesus' name, you make an impact on the world.

FORGIVENESS AND THE "UNFORGIVABLE"

Some actions and sins seem impossible to forgive. How can you forgive what seems to be unforgivable? How can you forgive in the midst of hurt that seems unbearable? We learn as we gaze at the Savior.

How could Jesus forgive those who crucified and mocked Him? These people did the unthinkable; they purposefully rejected and tortured Jesus. They even brazenly declared that the blood of His death be upon them and their children. How does a person respond to what is unforgivable?

I know what God wants me to do. He wants me to forgive. But what about those calloused individuals who hurt me to the core, who do so knowingly, and who do not even want my forgiveness. How can I give something that people don't even want? How did Corrie ten Boom forgive the guards who tormented her and killed her family? How does a mother forgive the drunk driver who kills her son and pleads innocent?

The mob before Jesus desperately needed forgiveness but they still completely focused on continuing in their sin. Jesus' words made no visible impact. The soldiers still gambled for His last shred of clothes, and the crowd mocked Him even more. Yet Jesus prayed for them.

I'm convinced everything Jesus did from the cross was meant for our example so that we, in taking up our crosses and following Him, can be triumphant. Forgiveness is a vital component of this process. We cannot get through these dark days without receiving Christ's words and allowing them to flow through us. The wounds and offenses of life pile up and weigh us down. If we don't find out how to unload our pain, hurts and, rejections, we will not make it through victoriously.

FORGIVENESS AND THE INVALUABLE SOUL

In His first words from the cross, Jesus gives us one of the great principles of forgiveness: "Father,

forgive them, for *they do not know what they do*"
(Luke 23:34). In today's terms we would say, "They
don't get it."

On first hearing, this statement seems wrong.
"Pastor, you don't understand," you might say. "They
knew exactly what they were doing when they hurt
me. It was premeditated. It was planned. They knew
they would hurt me, and they did it anyway."

Think of the person who stole your business. The
spouse who had the affair. The classmate who lied
about you in school. The coworker who stabbed
you in the back at work. In each case, the damage
was carried out according to plan. Your tormenters
knew exactly what they were doing.

But let's examine this issue more closely. Did the
crowd at the cross know what they were doing to
Jesus? Yes and no.

Did the Roman soldiers know they were crucifying a good man? Probably. But they didn't know He
was the King of kings. They were just doing their
job under orders.

Did Pilate know? Yes. His wife warned him.
But Pilate didn't know the whole story. He didn't

understand the concept of God in the flesh or a savior who dies.

What about Judas? Certainly he knew! Yes and no. When he saw what they were doing to Jesus, he tried to return the money. But he still didn't understand that Jesus was dying for him, and if he just held on forgiveness would come.

I am not saying these people are not guilty; they are guilty, just as you and I are guilty. This is not about guilt; it's about revelation. If we can see the truth about ourselves, it might be easier to forgive those who do the unforgivable to us.

Jesus knew that the people in the mob that day were blinded to what sin really is. They knew they were hurting Him, but they didn't know how much they were hurting themselves and those they loved. They acted purposefully, but didn't comprehend the magnitude of the sin they were committing.

People can't see or discern spiritual truth; the light isn't on in their hearts or spirits. This involves more than "knowing" in the sense of head knowledge; it's apprehending revelation or truth.

The cross enables us to see people differently, to

recognize they are in the same position as we are. The lost are not the enemy; they are the prize, and they are worth the battle to win them.

Jesus is saying, "I can forgive them because I know they aren't the enemy; they are being manipulated by evil, and I see them as worth saving." He did not win the battle with evil by giving us what we deserve, but by seeing the possibility of change within our hearts.

How does this principle play out in our lives when it comes to our responsibility to forgive? People need more than just hollow words of forgiveness. They need to hear us acknowledge, "I forgive you because I am like you. I need forgiveness too."

Forgiveness goes beyond saying, "I'll let you go because that's what is good for me." Genuine forgiveness says, "I forgive you because I believe you are worth it. Your value to me is more than the wrong you have done. I see the good in you, and I'm willing to fight for your redemption. People at their worst have yet to discover all the good they can live out once they are transformed by the Savior."

Spending time at the cross is the only way to understand how much we all need forgiveness. The best way to make forgiveness easier is to see that Jesus forgave us of our own unforgivable sin. Grasping this truth about ourselves makes it easier to forgive those who do the unforgivable to us.

The world expects us to be like them, but when we surprise them by fighting for them it can change their eternity. Forgiveness becomes the key to hardened hearts that breaks through satanic strongholds and reaches that person's core with the power of the gospel.

FORGIVENESS AND SELF-DISCOVERY

Perhaps we would not be so angry if we could see ourselves the way we really are. We don't know it all or have it all together. If we would admit we are not as good as we think we are or as righteous as we want people to think we are, we just might come to that place of obedience to the Holy Spirit's inner prompting where we let go of others' offenses against us and move on in victorious living.

Martin Luther King Jr. put it this way: "We must develop and maintain the capacity to forgive. He who is devoid of the power to forgive is devoid of the power to love. There is some good in the worst of us and some evil in the best of us. When we discover this, we are less prone to hate our enemies. The only way I know how to forgive is by taking the focus off of what others have done to me and to look at what Jesus has done for me."

The Book of Romans spells out just what Jesus has done: "For when we were still without strength, in due time Christ died for the ungodly. For scarcely for a righteous man will one die; yet perhaps for a good man someone would even dare to die. But God demonstrates His own love toward us, in that while we were still sinners, Christ died for us. Much more then, having now been justified by His blood, we shall be saved from wrath through Him. For if when we were enemies we were reconciled to God through the death of His Son, much more, having been reconciled, we shall be saved by His life" (Romans 5:6-10).

Here's how *The Message* puts it: "Christ arrives right on time to make this happen. He didn't, and doesn't, wait for us to get ready. He presented himself for this sacrificial death when we were far too weak and rebellious to do anything to get ourselves ready. And even if we hadn't been so weak, we wouldn't have known what to do anyway. We can understand someone dying for a person worth dying for, and we can understand how someone good and noble could inspire us to selfless sacrifice. But God put his love on the line for us by offering his Son in sacrificial death while we were of no use whatever to him" (Romans 5:6-8).

Every one of us needs a fresh revelation of Jesus' forgiveness. Being reminded of our fallen nature is humbling, and humility is a good place to begin when tackling the toughest issues of forgiveness.

There is no other way to live free from the darkness and the downward pull of pain and sin except to ask God to show us what He has done for us and then extend to others what He has given us. Stop trying to understand why "they did it." Look at Jesus. View the cross. Hear the Savior say, "I did this for you while you were at your worst. You didn't get it. You were blind. But now you see. So give them . . . Me."

No one gets through life without experiencing pain along the way. All of us have been broken by sin and blinded by our own desires and expectations.

Our challenge is to open our hearts to God's great grace and allow Him to free us from the bondage of unforgiveness and immature perspectives. We need to see others as God sees us, not try to make them understand how bad they are.

Forgiveness is easier when we remember that most of the time people don't know what they are really doing, just as we didn't understand ourselves when we hurt others. The best way to truly forgive is to spend time at the Cross. Remember how much He loved you and believed in you when you were at your worst. When your heart is filled afresh with the wonder of God's love and redemption, you can more easily forgive and bless others. You are simply following the example of what He has done for you. The act of forgiveness is as much for your benefit as for the people you are forgiving. It will open your heart to move beyond letting go of unforgiveness to willingly wanting others to be blessed with the Father's presence.

Take time today and fill your heart afresh with God's amazing forgiveness and goodness. Let His love heal your heart; then turn and give that love to someone else and watch what God does.

*Forgiveness becomes
the key to hardened
hearts that breaks
through spiritual
strongholds and reaches
that person's core with
the power of the gospel.*

From the
CROSS to
ETERNITY

TODAY YOU WILL BE WITH ME IN PARADISE

"THERE WERE ALSO TWO OTHERS, CRIMI-
NALS, led with Him to be put to death. And when
they had come to the place called Calvary, there they
crucified Him, and the criminals, one on the right
hand and the other on the left. ...And an inscription also was written over Him in letters of Greek,
Latin, and Hebrew: THIS IS THE KING OF THE
JEWS. Then one of the criminals who were hanged
blasphemed Him, saying, 'If you are the Christ, save

Yourself and us.' But the other, answering, rebuked him, saying, 'Do you not even fear God, seeing you are under the same condemnation? And we indeed justly, for we receive the due reward of our deeds; but this Man has done nothing wrong.' Then he said to Jesus, "Lord, remember me when You come into Your kingdom." And Jesus said to him, "Assuredly, I say to you, today you will be with Me in paradise" (Luke 23:32, 33, 38-43).

My approach to this word of Jesus takes more of a narrative form. Building a probable history or story on the relationships that surround the text makes the truths of this passage alive and personal.

COURTS OF LAWLESSNESS

The Bible gives a very detailed timeline of the last few days of Jesus' life. Especially on the last couple of days, we know where Jesus was and what He was doing almost every hour. God gives us this information for a reason. These details provide deeper truths about Jesus' redemption plan.

On the night of Jesus' arrest, He was praying in the Garden of Gethsemane. Judas came with a group of soldiers and priests who arrested Him. Jesus was bound and taken to the high priest's house where an illegal trial took place. The Jewish religious leaders condemned Jesus as a blasphemer for saying He was the Son of God.

All night long the men in charge beat and mocked Jesus. They taunted Him and baited Him to prophesy who had hit Him. Then they sent Him to Pilate, who in turn sent Him to King Herod.

"Then Herod, with his men of war, treated Him with contempt and mocked Him, arrayed Him in a gorgeous robe, and sent Him back to Pilate" (Luke 23:11).

Jesus was condemned to death by Pilate, the governor of Jerusalem. This is an important part of Jesus' story, because Pilate represented the power of Rome and the power of life and death.

The Jewish leaders shrewdly changed their charge from "blasphemer," their highest crime, to one of rebellion or attempting to overthrow the Roman government.

After Pilate interrogated Jesus, he took Him to the arch over the street and tried to release Him to the crowd. Pilate actually announced that he found nothing wrong or criminal in Jesus, and neither did Herod. But the Jewish leaders stirred up the crowd and demanded Jesus' death. And they didn't ask for just any death. They demanded the ultimate form of execution—crucifixion. They cried out, "Crucify Him! Crucify Him!" This went on for at least an hour and possibly for up to four hours.

Pilate was in a difficult place. He knew Jesus was an innocent Man—but the Jewish leaders threatened to cause a riot that would cost him his position as governor. Rome would not tolerate disruption or anyone who lets it happen.

Pilate brought out Jesus—beaten, bruised, and bleeding—and said again, "What evil has He done? I find no fault in him!" He hoped that a severe beating and mockery would be enough to satisfy the crowd. In Pilate's mind, Jesus' public influence was finished. Perhaps the people would be satisfied. But they wanted more. They wanted His death. Pilate turned Jesus over to the crowd and his soldiers to crucify Him. But before he did, he washed his hands—one of the greatest injustices in history.

PRISON OF THE RIGHTEOUS ONE

Where was Jesus during the time Pilate debated the Jewish leaders and then the mob?

He was in the praetorian prison, the walled fortress where Roman soldiers lived

Pilate lived and worked within a Roman garrison not far from the temple mount. Underneath this garrison was the praetorian or Roman prison where criminals who are condemned to death were held until their execution.

Tourists can still go to the prison cells that held the condemned. On the street they can see what is believed to be the arch where Pilate declared, "I find no fault in this Man," and where the crowd screamed, "Crucify Him!" In Latin the place is called the *Echo Homo* or the "Behold the Man" arch.

It is unlikely that Jesus was alone in that prison. Prisoners were often held in groups and chained to the wall. No one had a private cell. So who was with Him in prison? We know of three likely people: the two thieves who would be crucified with Him, and Barabbas.

"And they all cried out at once, saying, 'Away with this Man, and release to us Barabbas'—who had been thrown into prison for a certain rebellion made in the city, and for murder" (Luke 23:18, 19).

Murder was a crime punishable by crucifixion. Yet Barabbas is the one the people demand when Pilate offered to free Jesus as a gift to them.

"We want Barabbas!"

The two thieves were almost certainly there. They were both already condemned to death and would be crucified with Jesus. Perhaps they were all in the same cell. What conversations took place with Jesus, or about Jesus, while Pilate brought Him before the crowd?

CONDEMNED WITH THE SAVIOR

Jesus was beaten again and led to Golgotha to be crucified. He carried the beam of His own cross as far as He was able. Then Simon of Cyrene was forced to carry it for Him.

A great crowd, easily in the thousands, followed Jesus through the streets to Golgotha. The two condemned men were there as well, seeing and hearing everything.

"There were also two others, criminals, led with Him to be put to death" (Luke 23:32).

Who were these unnamed men? The Greek text implies they were members of the underworld—long-term, violent men of crime. Most likely, because of their sentence, they were cutthroat killers.

We do not know their names, but we know they had conversations with each other. They probably knew each other. They were sentenced to die at the same time, the same day as Jesus, and they were each crucified next to Him. They saw and heard the crowd and the Roman soldiers. They also saw the Savior and heard every word He spoke. You often see a different side of people when they are in pain. These men got to see what Jesus was really made of.

Both men were suffering and both were dying. On the outside they probably couldn't be distinguished from each other, but they represented two very different opinions of Jesus.

About the fifth hour, the thieves talked to Jesus.

The first criminal joined in mocking Him. His pain turned him against the Son of God.

"And the people stood looking on. But even the rulers with them sneered, saying, 'He saved others; let Him save Himself if He is the Christ, the chosen of God.' The soldiers also mocked Him, coming and offering Him sour wine, and saying, 'If You are the King of the Jews, save Yourself.' And an inscription also was written over Him in letters of Greek, Latin, and Hebrew: THIS IS THE KING OF THE JEWS. Then one of the criminals who were hanged blasphemed Him, saying, 'If You are the Christ, save Yourself and us'" (Luke 23:35-39).

"If you are a real King," he challenged, "save Yourself so You can save us from this fate."

The only recorded deeds and words of this man's life are his words of rejection toward the only One who could save Him.

On the surface his words appear as a question, but they are recorded as words of blasphemy: "If You are the Messiah, save Yourself and us." This man does not believe a king would allow himself to suffer so. Defeated kings have no followers in a world looking for easy power.

"You're a fake and You're defeated! Why don't You

just give it up and admit it? You can't save anyone. If You could, You would save Yourself and us. But it won't happen. You're no better than we are."

He seemed to want some form of salvation, but what he really wanted was just to escape. He was not sorry for his sins. He was just trying to get out of a mess. This man was a cynic, and many can identify with him.

There was no worship in his heart, no love for Jesus. There was only a life of sin, a life of being hurt and bearing the consequences. If anyone could have rescued him, he would not have changed. He'd have gone right back to his former life.

What a way to die.

The second criminal represents one of the great salvation stories in all of Scripture.

"But the other, answering, rebuked him, saying, 'Do you not even fear God, seeing you are under the same condemnation? And we indeed justly, for we receive the due reward of our deeds; but this Man has done nothing wrong.' Then he said to Jesus, 'Lord, remember me when You come into Your kingdom'" (Luke 23:40-42).

In the final hours of his wasted sinful life, a man with seemingly no hope met Jesus on the cross. Was any man in a more hopeless desperate situation? Did anyone ever deserve less from God?

Caught in crime, condemned and brutally crucified, the second criminal was dying in agony for crimes he freely admitted. He was a guilty man who was being justly punished. He deserved to die and knew it. But of all the people he could die with, he was with Jesus.

His life was in direct contrast to the Son of God. Jesus was sinless, innocent, and loving; this man was just the opposite. But two things happen that changed his life for eternity.

DYING REVELATION

First, this man heard Jesus pray to the Father to forgive His tormentors. If He would forgive them, perhaps He would forgive him! At the end of his failed life he had a glimmer of hope. Could forgiveness and grace be available for him?

Second, he had an opportunity to stand for Jesus, to express the seed of faith needed to come into relationship with the Savior.

When the first thief mocked Jesus, the second thief stood up for Him. He was not standing as a preacher or a theologian, but as a fellow sinner who said, "You can see this Jesus is different. He's not like us. You and I are guilty. We are receiving exactly what we deserve. This man is innocent; He has not sinned." These are deathbed words of faith from a criminal.

How did he come to this conclusion? Was it watching Jesus' response to Pilate and the crowd? Was it Jesus' courage or His grace? Was it His words or just the presence of the Holy Spirit?

The "how" doesn't matter. The important thing is that he understood and made the right response. He saw the difference. He knew Jesus was the spiritual King in spite of everything everyone else said.

If you stood at the cross for a while and listened to Jesus' words, you could see who He really is. This man saw a gracious King who was going to win somehow, someday. He prayed, "Lord, remember me when You come into Your Kingdom."

Notice that He called Jesus "Lord." He said, "I know You are the Messiah King and You will rule in Your Kingdom someday. Would You give me a place there? Would You remember me?" He didn't ask for much—just to be remembered when Jesus became King.

This is the most amazing example of faith in Jesus' character and grace in all of Scripture. All this man had seen was Jesus beaten and dying. Jesus hung next to him, a bloody mess, an awful sight to behold. The disciples were long gone; the whole world seemed against Him. The crowd jeered, spit, and roared like wild animals. Jesus could hardly talk. Yet this man, at the end of his wasted life, understood somehow.

"Jesus, You are King and You are Lord. You are going to rule and reign, and I want to be with You. I choose You even in death!"

This man never had the privilege of following Jesus, hearing His teaching, or seeing His miracles. But he understood the significance of Jesus' death and the promise of His renewed life. That is what mattered most. He had wasted his life. He was on the cross. He had hours, if not minutes, to live. In these last moments, he said, "Would You wipe away all of this for me? Would You have me in Your kingdom?"

PROMISED PARADISE

What was Jesus' response?

"And Jesus said to him, 'Assuredly, I say to you, today you will be with Me in Paradise'" (Luke 23:43).

His answer shows us three great salvation truths.

First, salvation is immediate. "*Today* you will be with Me."

Salvation and deliverance can take place in an instant. The moment you place your faith in Jesus and receive His forgiveness, you are forgiven. The Bible calls today the day of salvation. It is a now event. It is not about yesterday or tomorrow. It's today.

Second, salvation is personal.

The Greek rendering of Jesus' response is very important. The phrase means, "With Me in a very personal way." Jesus doesn't just forgive you, He comes beside you. He is your Savior and Friend. You are, in effect, the best and closest of friends. You and your Savior are together side by side as friends and eternal companions.

Wherever Jesus was going, the thief was going. Everything Jesus was going to inherit would be the thief's as well. Everything Jesus would win would be the thief's victory too.

Third, salvation promises the best of all possible futures.

Paradise is a very special word. It is only used three times in the Bible, and it describes heaven, the garden of the King. Heaven is the best thing God could make and a place no man can ruin. No sin can enter there. It's the best real estate in the universe.

"Paradise" was also used to describe the private garden of Babylon's great king. It was a beautiful garden, a cool and restful place where only friends and family were invited. It was the best place in the kingdom, available only to those few who occupied the king's inner circle.

Paradise was a place the thief had never been and could never hope to go. But the great King of kings was inviting him into the inner place. In one day he moved from something as close to hell as this world can offer—a cross—to paradise with Jesus. From rejection to intimacy with God.

The second thief took Jesus at His word. Despite his agony, he waited with hope and faith for the end.

God placed this wretch in the prison with Jesus, on the road to Calvary with Jesus and on the cross next to Jesus. Then, in a moment, he woke up in heaven with Jesus. What he thought was the worst day of his life became the best day of his life. This unnamed thief went down in history as one of the greatest victories of all eternity.

SALVATION'S GIFT

Life may not be very good to you right now. You may have made a mess of things and are living through some undeserved or even deserved pain. But there is good news. God's grace is greater than your sins.

"For if by the one man's offense death reigned through the one, much more those who receive abundance of grace and of the gift of righteousness will reign in life through the One, Jesus Christ. Therefore, as through one man's offense judgment came to all men, resulting in condemnation, even so through one Man's righteous act the free gift came to all men, resulting in justification of life. For as by one man's disobedience many were made sinners, so also by one Man's obedience many will be made righteous. Moreover the law entered that the offense might abound. But where sin abounded, grace abounded much more, so that as sin reigned in death, even so grace might reign through righteousness to eternal life through Jesus Christ our Lord" (Romans 5:17-21).

Whatever you have done, God's grace through Christ is greater and stronger. It is never too late to ask Jesus for help. God's grace will receive you and forgive you, even if you wait until the end of your life. Don't carry your secret sins and shame another minute. Give them to Jesus. He will take them and He will take you. The key is to turn to Him, not away from Him.

Both thieves were in need of God's grace. Only one turned to Jesus for help; the other turned against Him. You and I are not here by accident; God calls and draws us, and He bids us to respond today.

Perhaps the most amazing word Jesus spoke to that second thief was *today*. Even now He says, "Good news! Not someday—today! Faster and sooner than you think. Today you and I will be in paradise together."

God is here today, and He is working today. You can be changed today!

You may have come to a place where you realize that your life is far off course and you are paying for your mistakes and sins. The Cross declares that it is never too late to give your life to Christ and become His follower. There is hope for you no matter how bad you think you have been. So take your stand with Jesus; He wants you to be His.

Above all, remember that God can do the miraculous. He created you to rule and reign with Him. In one day He can turn your world right-side up again. So hold on—victory is closer than you think.

The moment you place your faith in Jesus and receive His forgiveness, you are forgiven. The Bible calls today the day of salvation. It is a now event. It is not about yesterday or tomorrow. It's today.

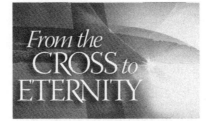

BEHOLD YOUR SON

"NOW THERE STOOD BY THE CROSS OF *Jesus His mother, and His mother's sister, Mary the wife of Clopas, and Mary Magdalene. When Jesus therefore saw His mother, and the disciple whom He loved standing by, He said to His mother, 'Woman, behold your son!' Then He said to the disciple, 'Behold your mother!' And from that hour that disciple took her to his own home"* (John 19:25-27).

Of all the last words of Jesus, His message to His mother and best friend may be the most overlooked. Yet it is one of the most compassionate and practical words He ever gave.

Jesus had been betrayed and forsaken by His friends. All of Jerusalem demanded His death. He had been beaten and led through the mocking crowd to the place where criminals were crucified. Most painful of all, He cannot feel the presence of His Father. As He hung crucified, He carries the weight of the world's sin.

After hours of suffering and mockery, He looked down from the cross and saw His mother standing next to His closest disciple. He said to Mary, "Woman, behold your son!" To John he said, "Behold your mother!"

The original Greek emphasizes not only the words Jesus spoke but also the intensity and the compassion of how He said them. His directive command is based on unfathomable love.

It is as though Jesus said, "Mother, open your eyes wide and look at John. See him in a new way. He is now your son. Receive him and love him as a son.

"John—my friend—open your eyes and see My mother Mary as I do. Look closely. See her enormous value. Take her as your own mother. Care for each other."

The beautiful truth of this narrative is that John and Mary grasped the significance of His words. From that moment Mary went to live with John, and he cared for her until her death many years later, probably in Ephesus.

A New Family

The theme of Jesus' first words from the cross is simple: Relationships are vital for endurance and victory. Lasting, trusting relationships are the most valuable treasures in life. They empower us to make it through our trials. But before we can understand and apply what Jesus said, we need to remember how special His relationship was with both Mary and John.

To be the mother of Jesus was the highest honor that could be given to a woman. We cannot fully understand the great mystery of how much Mary loved Jesus, but it had to be one of the greatest mother/son relationships of all time. It is totally inadequate to merely say that Jesus loved Mary and that she loved Him.

It had to have been heart-rending for Mary to

stand at the cross and see her Son, the holy and loving Messiah, dying such a torturous death. But somehow she mustered the courage to be there for Him—to stand beneath Him, where He could glance down at her for the comfort of her presence.

The Bible tells us that John was the disciple Jesus loved. Jesus loves us all, as He did all of His disciples, yet John had a special place in His heart. They shared a holy friendship, an understanding of hearts and bonding of souls that was unique among Jesus' relationships.

By the time Jesus went to the cross, most of His followers had run away or were standing at a safe distance. But Mary and John were right there next to the soldiers. They saw the nails pounded into Christ's flesh. They heard the priests mocking and the crowd taunting, yet they stood together as an island of support in a sea of hatred. Looking at Jesus, they tried to comprehend His suffering and encourage Him at the same time.

Now Jesus spoke and gave those He loved most to each other. "See each other in a new way," He says. "I want you to be a family, to take the love you have for Me and give it to each other. I am asking you to share a richer life together."

LIFE-GIVING RELATIONSHIPS

So what truth is Jesus speaking to us from the cross?

First, don't let your trials cave in on you. Let's be honest; difficult times can bring fear. Fear can bring discouragement, and discouragement can lead to isolation. It's easy to lose the battle when you're isolated.

Jesus' words to Mary and John reveal the necessity of not letting dark trials isolate us from other people. We must stay connected, even in our times of sorrow and suffering. We need the help of others to make it through life's challenges victoriously.

Our natural tendency is to withdraw into ourselves when our pain reaches a certain threshold. Sometimes withdrawal is necessary. But when the level of our disconnect becomes too great, we cut ourselves off from the help God makes available to us in the body of Christ.

Jesus' pain was beyond anything we can imagine,

and it could have driven Him to disconnect. He had every reason to withdraw and totally focus on His own problems and pain. But He didn't. He refused to let life overwhelm Him. Even though He was dying for the sins of the world, He was not too busy to take care of His mother and His close friend—to address their needs and fears.

Jesus illustrated a powerful Cross principle: When life is hardest, spending time with and serving others will strengthen us. When you long to pull away and focus on yourself, God calls you to help others. And as you reach out, you find new strength and victory.

Think about how this principle plays havoc with the schemes of the enemy of our souls. Jesus is telling us not to let the evil one force us into retreat or isolation, but to recognize our need for others in the body of Christ. When we stay connected, we experience victory.

Consider 1 John 3:13, 14: "Do not marvel, my brethren, if the world hates you. We know that we have passed from death to life, because we love the brethren. He who does not love his brother abides in death."

Matthew 18:20 offers a similar message: "For where two or three are gathered together in My name, I am there in the midst of them."

Think of it! Where two or three of God's people gather together, Christ is there among us to provide what we need. Is it any wonder that during our times of greatest pain the enemy tempts us to withdraw? If he can isolate us, he can depress us. And if we allow depression to have its way, it will drag us down. Isolation magnifies our problems and facilitates our fears.

But that is not the way to victory. Jesus teaches us that we need others to get through life. We are not called to hurt alone or to win alone. We are God's family, and the network of life-giving relationships we develop in that family is our secret to overcoming.

GETTING BEYOND SELF

No matter what you're going through, remember that life is more than yourself and your needs. It's in giving that you receive and in fellowship that you find strength. As we come together we find relief from the stresses of life.

This principle of reaching beyond self is plainly stated in Hebrews 10:19-25: "Therefore, brethren, having boldness to enter the Holiest by the blood of Jesus, by a new and living way which He consecrated for us, through the veil, that is, His flesh, and having a High Priest over the house of God, let us draw near with a true heart in full assurance of faith, having our hearts sprinkled from an evil conscience and our bodies washed with pure water. Let us hold fast the confession of our hope without wavering, for He who promised is faithful. And let us consider one another in order to stir up love and good works, not forsaking the assembling of ourselves together, as is the manner of some, but exhorting one another, and so much the more as you see the Day approaching."

What does it mean to assemble ourselves together? It extends beyond a local church's schedule of services or a small group Bible study. A fuller picture is one of believers joining together in fellowship—eating, sharing, laughing, crying, or, sometimes, just sitting together in silence.

Everyone gets lonely. But what we do with our loneliness will affect every aspect of our lives. Dag

Hammarskjold, the second Secretary-General of the United Nations, said: "Pray that your loneliness may spur you into finding something to live for, great enough to die for." Being willing to die for someone gives you strength to live—and to conquer the worst the world can throw at you. Through completely giving yourself to Christ and His family, you will lose your natural tendency toward selfishness and become truly empowered.

I believe the example that Jesus gave us was part of His victory on the cross. As He suffered alone, He felt forsaken by the Father and by His friends. But He didn't let His agony drive Him inward. He used His pain and loneliness to encourage others. He showed us that victory depends on thinking of others and giving to others when you would rather think about yourself. We must stay connected, even when we are called to go through the fire. In those connections, we find the strength to overcome.

WIDENING THE CIRCLE

Jesus loved Mary and John, and they loved Him. Now Jesus said to them, "You need to change the way you see each other. Widen your circle of love." There could be no love like that shared by Jesus and Mary. Yet Jesus was saying, "Mother, you need another son." And to the disciple He loved deeply, He was saying, "John, you're My best friend, but you need a family. So here is My mother. Now she is your mother too."

With these instructions, Jesus encouraged His family and friends to connect with others—not just with Him. Simply put, Jesus loves us enough to command us to love others.

No single person's love is enough. If you love someone, you want others to love them. And, you want them to love others. Through a multiplicity of relationships, love succeeds and grows.

Everyone needs Jesus, and no one else can take His place. But everyone needs people who will communicate His love into their lives. Who are the people in your life who need a wider circle of Christ-honoring relationships?

Mom, your children need friends. Husband, your wife needs friends. Spouses need to schedule "girlfriends' night out" and "guys' night out." God created us to find balance and strength in community. We need to learn how to grow emotionally and spiritually healthy through relationships with others.

Perhaps the most challenging example of this principle is when a father releases a daughter to a husband. When my daughter, Jessica, told me she was marrying Mark Sheffield, I struggled a bit. I was no longer the "go to" guy. My phone calls were no longer returned as quickly. When people asked me how the wedding plans were coming, I would say, "I'm the last to know!"

Then I remembered that I had prepared her for this since she was a little girl. Beginning some twenty years ago on our "dad and daughter dates" I would tell her, "Someday someone is going to love you and cherish you like I do, and I want to get you ready."

Love is not ownership; it is a foundation on which to build healthy, connected lives. It involves careful, watchful protection, knowing that others' ultimate success or failure can depend on the quality of friendships they develop. Your loved ones need your permission and blessing to develop healthy, spiritual friendships. Opening our horizons to new life-giving relationships makes all of us stronger.

The first of Jesus' last words from the cross reminds us that we must keep building a genuine spiritual community in our lives. Our survival depends on it. The world pulls people apart, breaks them down, and caves in on them behind locked doors. But Jesus says, "Don't be afraid. You are not alone, and together you can be victorious."

Trials are part of God's plan. But even though we know God is at work during these difficult times, it is easy to let the lies of the enemy get a grip on us. When we are hurting we typically withdraw into ourselves and miss the strength that comes from fully developed spiritual relationships. Perhaps your trial has led you into isolation and an unhealthy self-focus. Problems are clouding your vision. Today God wants you to know that He understands and will help you re-engage in His master plan for your life. Sometimes the best place to start is right outside your door. Look around and find someone to help. Reaching out to others may seem the very opposite of what you think you need, but when you do it as a step of faith God's presence will flow into your heart.

God did not call us to live in isolation. You are never closer to the heart of God than when you help others connect in a deeper relationship to Christ and with others. So today take a moment and look for the "God opportunity" of helping others with their problems. Remember, something powerful happens when you share your life with others.

Relationships are vital for endurance and victory. Lasting, trusting relationships are the most valuable treasures in life. They empower us to make it through our trials.

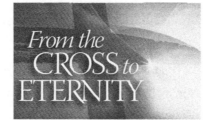

From the
CROSS *to*
ETERNITY

MY GOD,
MY GOD,
WHY HAVE YOU
FORSAKEN ME?

"**F**ROM NOON TO THREE, THE WHOLE *earth was dark. Around mid-afternoon Jesus groaned out of the depths, crying loudly, 'Eli, Eli, lama sabachthani?' which means, 'My God, my God, why have you abandoned me?'"* (Matthew 27:45, 46, *The Message*).

In his book *Hard Sayings of Jesus,* F. F. Bruce discusses seventy of the hardest sayings of the Savior to understand. The last one Bruce considers is this statement, which he describes as "the hardest of all the hard statements."

No statement is more mysterious than this one. The problem is not with the words themselves, but with their larger meaning and with the question of why Jesus would say them.

A story is told of Martin Luther as he was studying this text one day. For hours he sat and stared at the words. He said nothing, he wrote nothing; he just silently pondered Jesus' words. Suddenly he stood up and exclaimed, "God forsaking God? How can it be?"

Indeed, how can the Father forsake His own Son? This is holy ground, and His words are here for a reason. We need to hear them in our own language and connect them with our own experience.

LIGHT IN THE DARKNESS

Matthew describes the halfway point of Jesus' last hours on the cross as a time of darkness. A physical darkness descended over the earth for three hours, from noon to 3 o'clock in the afternoon. At noon, normally the brightest time of the day, great darkness shrouded everything. It was so spectacular that Matthew noted the hour it came and the hour it left. It was not an eclipse or a cloud. It was darkness itself—the kind of darkness you can feel. The darkness spoke of evil, heaviness of spirit and death.

The Gospels indicate that silence came with the darkness. Before that moment, just about everyone was talking—the thieves, the Roman soldiers, the priests, and the mob. But when darkness came, no one moved. No one spoke. For once, the profane soldiers stopped their swearing. The mockers grew silent. The atmosphere was as if an evil force had subdued the earth. It was like the dark laughter of hell; hell thought it had won, and Satan felt like he had conquered.

For three hours the darkness remained, and it felt like the end of the world. Every eye was on the cross. This was the world's great wake-up call to the spiritual warfare that centers on the cross.

HIS SEPARATION, OUR RESTORATION

Then Jesus spoke four words in Aramaic. When translated, they are some of the most baffling words in the English language: "My God, my God, why have You forsaken me?"

It is significant that Matthew first writes these words in Aramaic, the language of the people. He doesn't use Hebrew or Greek, but the common man's language.

Why did Jesus say that? I am convinced it was how He felt at that moment. He wasn't preaching or expressing a spiritual reality about the people around Him. He wasn't trying to get attention or produce a dramatic effect. Jesus Christ was talking to His Father. His heart was broken, and it was more than He could bear.

These words form both a question and a plea. Jesus is at the bottom of the blackest spiritual and emotional pit. But His cry didn't signify a defeated Savior or even a momentary failure in an otherwise perfect, eternally established plan of salvation. Jesus did not fail. In fact, in just a few moments He would declare victory.

This is the cry of the divine Son as His Father turned His back on Him. For the first and only time in eternity past or present, Jesus' intimate relationship with His Father was broken.

We cannot fathom the shock of separation Jesus experienced. Only one word defines this ultimate expression of being forsaken: hell.

The phrase "God-forsaken" usually refers to some barren, desert place where nothing can grow and no one can live. But those places are not God-forsaken. They may be dry and barren, but if you look closely there is life and, more importantly, there is God. To be truly God-forsaken is to experience something worse than death. It is existence without God's presence, love, and hope. It is hell. And in the darkness on this day, Jesus felt what it is like when God removes His presence.

Ultimately, Hell is hell because God is not there. It's the only place God is not and will not be. Being in that place is an unbearable existence, since it is devoid of true life. It is the second death.

And yet, we encounter hints of hell in this life. Religion without the knowledge of a loving, faithful Heavenly Father is a kind of living hell. Atheism or agnosticism denies any ability to know God and creates a kind of hell. Even prideful rejection of God's love gives a taste of hell as we discover just how futile and empty all of life's pursuits are without His blessing and fulfillment.

In this moment of Jesus' separation, His statement offers us another clue to His agony. As many have pointed out, this is the only time Jesus addressed God as "My God." Everywhere else He called Him "Father." But here He said, "My God" because the Father/Son relationship was broken.

So why does the Holy Spirit let us in on this moment? Because it shows us what sin really is: separation. Sin is evil because it separates us from God. At times it may look harmless, but it is terrible in its consequences. Sin has a price, and the greatest price is that a holy God cannot fellowship with sin. Sin always brings a gap that is greater than we can imagine.

"For the wages of sin is death, but the gift of God is eternal life in Christ Jesus our Lord" (Romans 6:23).

ULTIMATE PENALTY, IMMEASURABLE GIFT

God the Father turned away because Jesus was bearing the penalty of sin for the world. As John the Baptist rightly declared when he first saw Jesus, "Behold! The Lamb of God who takes away the sin of the world" (John 1:29).

One of the most powerful Old Testament pictures of Christ's atoning sacrifice is described in Leviticus 16. On the Day of Atonement, two goats were chosen. One was slaughtered and its blood sprinkled on the ark of the covenant in the tabernacle's Holy of Holies as a symbolic atonement for Israel's sin. Jesus, of course, is our eternal sacrifice and His blood has forever atoned for humanity's sin. The second goat, the scapegoat, was taken by a man deep into the wilderness away from the camp of Israel. This scapegoat also speaks of our Savior.

On the cross, Jesus was sin—the sin of the whole world. He was my sin, your sin, Republican sin, Democrat sin, independent sin, capitalist sin, communist sin, men's sin, women's sin, teenagers' sin, drug dealers' and religious hypocrites' sin, prostitutes' and child abusers' sin, preachers' and lawyers' and politicians' and grocers' and street sweepers' sins—all sin for all time and in all environments.

And as much as the Father loved the Son, He

could not stay by Him at that moment. Jesus was on His own.

"He is despised and rejected by men, a Man of sorrows and acquainted with grief. And we hid, as it were, our faces from Him. He was despised, and we did not esteem Him. Surely He has borne our griefs and carried our sorrows; yet we esteemed Him stricken, smitten by God, and afflicted. But He was wounded for our transgressions, He was bruised for our iniquities; the chastisement for our peace was upon Him, and by His stripes we are healed. All we like sheep have gone astray; we have turned, every one, to his own way; and the Lord has laid on Him the iniquity of us all" (Isaiah 53:3-6).

Jesus not only bore sin's penalty, but also the scars, the pain, and the damage it brings. For the redeemed, the picture is one of painful self-acknowledgment, gratitude, and eternal hope. For the world, the picture is loathsome. The world hates the cross. Unbelievers instinctively know it represents not only the love of God, but also the reality of sin and its penalty.

Jesus was alone—more alone than anyone has ever been—and He needed to express His pain to the Father. He felt the absence of the intimate fellowship with God He had always known, and He was asking the Father: "Why am I alone now?"

Jesus bore our grief on the cross. He took our sins, our rejection, and our loneliness. He took our physical sickness, our mental illness, and our sorrow. We need to see this truth front and center today and understand the enormity of what He accomplished on our behalf. He took our rejection and the pain of being despised and unwanted. And now, because of Him, no one can take away our immeasurable worth.

NEVER ALONE

Everyone experiences times of darkness. The call to follow Christ is not a call to a trouble-free life. Darkness came to Jesus, and darkness will come to us. Satan will not let us serve God untried; he will try to break our hearts.

Jesus is Lord and His victory is secure, but until His kingdom comes He calls us to follow Him through valleys and times of personal darkness. We are engaged in spiritual warfare, and the enemy is working his worst to rob, steal, and destroy lives.

At times we feel God's great presence; at other times everything looks dark and the weight of oppression comes. God's Word tells us to expect times when evil will abound and our faith will be tested. Weariness will tempt us to give up and give in to fear and discouragement.

"No one should be shaken by these afflictions; for you yourselves know that we are appointed to this. For, in fact, we told you before when we were with you that we would suffer tribulation, just as it happened, and you know. For this reason, when I could no longer endure it, I sent to know your faith, lest by some means the tempter had tempted you, and our labor might be in vain" (1 Thessalonians 3:3-5).

No one wants or enjoys trials. But if we are going to follow Christ we must follow Him through them, knowing that God is with us even when we can't feel Him. Jesus promised that He will never, ever forsake or leave us. "And lo, I am with you always, even to the end of the age" (Matthew 28:20).

He is always there. Sometimes He sends a person. Sometimes He sends a word. Sometimes you wait for Him in the night. But He is there.

One of the hardest times to sense God's leading is when we are completely alone and it seems everyone we counted on let us down. During those times in my life, I have discovered that God is there and He is more than enough. Those moments of discovery produce greater confidence and peace than I can find anywhere else in life.

But, an even harder time is when you feel God is not there for you. The roll call of those who have felt that way includes some of the greatest champions in history. Job could not feel God; Moses was sure God had abandoned him in the desert. Joshua felt forsaken by God when he lost what he thought was a simple battle with Ai after the great Jericho victory. If you feel God has withdrawn His presence, remember He is still there. He is at work in your life, even though you can't feel Him. During these times of solitude, He is taking your faith deeper.

Jesus took your loneliness so He could always be with you. You will never go through anything alone. Jesus has been there first, and He is with you now. Remember, the cross is empty and the Resurrection won eternity's greatest battle.

SHARING HIS LIGHT

Darkness is temporary, but victory is eternal. Darkness is a lie; it doesn't have the power to win. Jesus is the light, and where the light shines, darkness flees. We are the light of the world, and His Spirit is in us. Truth sets us free and gives us what offers freedom to others.

The darkness at Calvary had a beginning and an end—three hours. I believe this detail is included to show us that there is a time limit to the darkness of our soul. Times of darkness can have a thousand purposes for your life and for others. But darkness is never the final destiny or habitation for the believer.

We are children of the light, and the Sun of righteousness always arises with healing and victory. Jesus is still Lord, and God is with us. The church is alive and God's promises are secure. The goodness of God invades the pain of life.

God calls us to hold on and rest on His unchanging grace. As the old hymn states: "On Christ, the solid Rock, I stand; All other ground is sinking sand... When darkness veils His lovely face, I rest on His unchanging grace; In every high and stormy gale, my anchor holds within the veil."

God's presence surrounds us 24/7. He is the faithful Savior who walks by your side and will never leave you. And today, no matter what you face, you can be sure that Jesus, the Glory of heaven, is coming again. We have one less day until our own resurrection and the Second Coming. One less day of pain, tears, and loneliness. One less day when creation groans under sin's burden.

The clock is ticking, so keep your eyes on God. Don't grow weary and surrender to darkness and despair. Give someone an embrace of encouragement. Share a promise and a good word. We are not going down. We're going forward toward that great Day of the Lord.

"Behold, I tell you a mystery: We shall not all sleep, but we shall all be changed—in a moment, in the twinkling of an eye, at the last trumpet. For the trumpet will sound, and the dead will be raised incorruptible, and we shall be changed. For this corruptible must put on incorruption, and this mortal must put on immortality. So when this corruptible has put on incorruption, and this mortal has put on immortality, then shall be brought to pass the saying that is written: 'Death is swallowed up in victory.'

"'O death, where is your sting? O Hades, where is your victory?' The sting of death is sin, and the strength of sin is the law. But thanks be to God, who gives us the victory through our Lord Jesus Christ. Therefore, my beloved brethren, be steadfast, immovable, always abounding in the work of the Lord, knowing that your labor is not in vain in the Lord" (1 Corinthians 15:51-58).

Be assured of this: Jesus gave His Word that He will never leave you, and He always keeps His Word. Sometimes you feel His glory. At other times He is standing behind you in the darkness—but He is still there. Don't despair today. You are not alone. If you are going through a painful, dark moment, reach out and talk to someone. You will find others have felt this way too, and on the other side a fresh outpouring of His presence awaits.

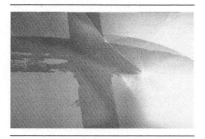

*Jesus took your loneliness
so that He could always
be with you. You will
never go through
anything alone. Jesus has
been there first,
and He is with you now.*

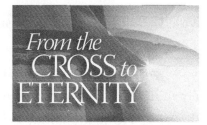

From the
CROSS *to* ETERNITY

I THIRST

"*AFTER THIS, JESUS, KNOWING THAT ALL things were now accomplished, that the Scripture might be fulfilled, said, 'I thirst!' Now a vessel full of sour wine was sitting there; and they filled a sponge with sour wine, put it on hyssop, and put it to His mouth*" (John 19:28, 29).

Few things speak of humanity more than thirst. When Jesus says, "I thirst," He's also saying, "I'm human and I need help." In the Greek, "I thirst" is just one word, but that word must have startled the crowd! Jesus—the One who had done miracles, who had confronted the most powerful religious leaders in the land, who had raised Lazarus from the dead—was now asking for help. This word from the cross divided the crowd and intensified their examination of who Jesus was.

This is the only time Jesus ever asked for help in public. Equally significant, His words seem contrary to the very promise He made about being Living Water and offering himself so that no one need thirst again. But this confirmation of Jesus' humanity with His divinity assures us that our Savior intimately connects with each of us. By voicing His vulnerability and need, He spoke for every anguished soul who struggles in this life.

EVERYONE NEEDS HELP

Few needs are more vital than the need for water. Thirst focuses all of our energy and attention on something that is absolutely essential to our lives.

On the cross, Jesus was thirsty. The beatings, the bleeding, and the pain caused Him to be dehydrated. He was pushed to the limits of survival, and His body screamed out for water. Just a few drops would help Him finish His task.

The timeline of the Crucifixion places this scene toward the end of Jesus' time on the cross. Until this moment He has been a tower of strength. Then, the King of Glory asks for help.

His disciples and His enemies alike must have been shocked when they heard His words. Those who loved Him could have wondered if He was finally breaking under the strain. Those who hated Him might have thought they had finally succeeded in rendering Him powerless.

Jesus had prayed for forgiveness for those who were crucifying Him. He had blessed the thief next to Him. He had felt the loneliness of separation from His Heavenly Father's presence. In it all, He remained strong and unyielding. He was almost there, almost at the apex of His mission. Only "It is finished" remained.

Then, for the first time, it was as though Jesus was saying, "I'm human and I'm in need. Would someone give Me a little water?" Jesus had asked the Samaritan woman to give Him a drink of water, but He did not say to her, "I am thirsty." His request was ultimately for her benefit. Jesus was hungry at the end of His fast in the wilderness when He was tempted by the devil, but angels took care of Him there.

This request from the cross stands apart from anything He had experienced. Why would He ask for help now? Because He was human, and humans have limitations. Jesus was one of us. He was in agony, and the human side of Him needed help. He wasn't ashamed or afraid to express His need. Revealing His human side was part of God's redeeming plan.

A dear woman once asked me, "Pastor, when did Jesus become God?" And I said, "He was always God. The wonder is that He became human."

Jesus became one of us. His humanity doesn't lessen our love for Him; it opens our heart to love Him more and gives us hope. It demonstrates that He understands us and relates to whatever we are facing. We can make it through life with Him at our side.

EVERY NEED HAS A PURPOSE

The Bible tells us that Jesus felt the same needs and emotions we experience. "For we do not have a High Priest who cannot sympathize with our weaknesses, but was in all points tempted as we are, yet without sin. Let us therefore come boldly to the throne of grace, that we may obtain mercy and find grace to help in time of need" (Hebrews 4:15, 16).

In the Greek, the term translated "time of need" refers to a strategic moment of need. It implies that our need is not meaningless or just coincidental. When we experience need, God reaches out to us, shares in that need, and responds when we ask for help.

Our "time of need" means that God is working His plan through our human limitations. In the midst of our problems, trials, and battles, He is working for us and through us. He uses our inabilities and failures to work His redemption plan.

Think about it. God is at work in your limitations. He is active in your thirst. In your weakness, He is carrying out His divine purposes. This holds true even in God's greatest mission—the Great Commission. We don't win the world to Christ through our victories alone, but also through our limitations. He takes our weaknesses and shows himself strong through them. Being honest and daring to ask for help is part of His redemption plan.

Our needs and weaknesses have purpose, and asking for help is not a sign of failure. Was Jesus a failure? Surely the enemies of Christ thought He was, especially when He asked for water. Even the disciples saw His crucifixion as a failure and a defeat. But Jesus was not a failure. Instead, He was winning the battle against evil and drawing people to Himself.

When you reach the end of yourself, you are not a failure. You may say, "I don't have what it takes. I've come up short." But that doesn't mean you are failing. Instead, you are in a perfect position for God to take your need and weakness and use them to bring victory in your life.

Paul gave the Corinthian church perspective concerning how God uses our weakness when he wrote: "For you see your calling, brethren, that not many wise according to the flesh, not many mighty, not many noble, are called. But God has chosen the foolish things of the world to put to shame the wise, and God has chosen the weak things of the world to put to shame the things which are mighty; and the base things of the world and the things which are despised God has chosen, and the things which are not, to bring to nothing the things that are, that no flesh should glory in His presence" (1 Corinthians 1:26-29).

God is not looking for people who are strong or great in themselves; He is looking for those who have the courage to live honestly and openly while leaning on Jesus.

EVERY BURDEN CAN BE SHARED

Being honest and real is not a sign of weakness. Instead, it reveals that a person understands grace and redemption. Christians aren't perfect; they are in the process of being perfected. Being a Christian does not mean I have no needs. It means I am not afraid to ask for help. The staff members at our church are all committed to this principle: We can't succeed alone, and we can't fail if we ask for help.

Galatians 6:2-5 makes this fascinating and, at first glance, contradictory statement: "Bear one another's burdens, and so fulfill the law of Christ. For if anyone thinks himself to be something, when he is nothing, he deceives himself. But let each one examine his own work, and then he will have rejoicing in himself alone, and not in another. For each one shall bear his own load."

In this passage, Paul uses two different words for burdens. One refers to the burdens we help each other carry—the situations that demean and ravage life. Paul says that the enemy will try to ravage and destroy those among us. At that point we need to help carry one another's burden. The other word used refers to our individual spiritual responsibilities, the "burdens" for which each of us is responsible and no one else.

God intends for us to help each other with life's burdens and to live truthfully and compassionately toward each other. When we are honest and ask for help, miracles can happen. I have witnessed them firsthand.

Our church reached a point where we needed a large amount of money to prepare for future outreach. There were no resources left in the budget, so the deacons and I prayed. As we did, I felt impressed by God to go to a few people and ask for help.

It is not my nature to approach people personally with a church need. But in obedience, I shared the situation with a few friends. "Can you see this need?" I asked. "Does this stir your heart?"

These people were not insulted or in any way threatened by what I did. Every one of them was willing to be involved. Their most frequent response was, "Thanks for asking. We didn't know you needed us."

Not Every Need Finds a Visible Response

In a perfect world, we find plenty of help with our burdens. But we don't live in a perfect world. Asking for help doesn't always bring about the needed response. Sometimes people let us down.

Remember Matthew 27:47-49? Jesus' request for water was met with a mocking reference to the prophet Elijah and the offer of a sponge full of sour wine.

Being honest with your problems and battles comes with a risk. You might take that risk only to have people let you down. As painful as that may be, it is part of God's plan of winning the world and glorifying God through your struggles.

A crucial moment of your life and an ultimate testing time for your faith is when you dare to reach out and others let you down. Instead of giving Jesus water, they gave Him vinegar. You can drink only a little vinegar, and it will physically cost you as much as it helps. If you try to drink too much, it can kill you.

There are different avenues of false help in life. Sometimes people fail you unintentionally. You ask for help, but they just don't understand. Or they think they are helping when they are really hurting you. That's the "vinegar variety" crowd.

Sometimes people deliberately try to hurt you in your need. These are the "Elijah-watchers" at the cross. "Leave Him alone; let's see if Elijah will help Him now," they mutter. "Let's see who this Jesus really is." These people stand back in your moment of need and merely watch to see if God is real enough to intervene on your behalf.

Whatever your situation, remember that God is at work, even while the enemy is working. And in the midst of it all, the world is watching. What we do when we hurt is part of God's plan of showing himself to be the real solution to every problem. Sometimes God wants you to simply rest in Him, even though others don't see the answer to the problem.

Look again at Galatians 6:2-5. Paul says that people can help you, but there are some things people cannot or will not do. When these situations come, you need to lean on God. He wants us to cling to Him and let Him carry us.

EVERY VICTORY IS ASSURED

A great breakthrough in your life will come when you discover that you and Jesus are a majority and no one can take you from His hand. When you are anchored in Him, you will not fold—not today, not this week, not in this lifetime. Jesus got you this far; He will get you through to tomorrow.

In Christ, you are stronger than you think. You can climb the mountain and walk through the valley. You can overcome bitterness and failure. Hold on to His love today as you look in faith toward tomorrow. I am sure the crowd at the cross expected Jesus to fold. They thought He would lash out and curse them and give up on them. But He didn't.

Sometimes people push us so they can discover what we really believe. People are watching us right now. They are looking at us and saying, "They're in the same predicament we are. I wonder if they will fold. I wonder if this Jesus thing is real."

The world's questions sometimes echo our own. Even when we know Jesus is with us, we find ourselves asking, "Can I do this? Will this work? I don't think I have what it takes." But if you have Jesus, you have what it takes. You were not made for "almost victory," and you were not created to be "almost righteous."

In order to win the spiritual battle for Christ in these last days, we have to be different from the world. We need strength to love when we are not loved, to forgive when we are hurt, and to bless when we are cursed. Even in times of great thirst, we can gain strength from the Living Water who is always sufficient.

Living openly as saved but incomplete Christians is challenging. People will sometimes misunderstand and even criticize us, but remember that the benefit of serving Christ is far greater than the cost. What matters most is that we live in honesty and genuineness before others. Our openness does not stem from a pride that says, "Look what I've done" but from a peaceful humility that says, "I'm still incomplete, but I'm pressing on toward God's goal for my life." As the familiar saying states: "Be patient with me. God is not finished with me yet."

Put this lesson into practice today by opening your heart to someone who needs to know that serving God does not equate with perfection. Life is not just a straight line upward; it includes a few valleys and setbacks. Share your personal journey, including your needs, so others can know how to help. People cannot meet all our needs, but Jesus often uses them to give us comfort and strength. And He will always be there to make a way where there seems no way.

Today is also a good day to help someone else who is thirsty. A cup of water given in Jesus' name will never lose its reward. So open up and let God use you to bless others. Life is give and take. God is using you—and others—to accomplish His plans.

God is not looking for people who are strong or great in themselves; He is looking for those who have the courage to live honestly and openly while leaning on Jesus.

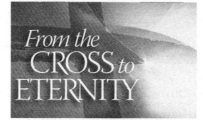

From the
CROSS *to*
ETERNITY

IT IS FINISHED!

"**S**O WHEN JESUS HAD RECEIVED THE SOUR *wine, He said, 'It is finished!' And bowing His head, He gave up His spirit. Therefore, because it was the Preparation Day, that the bodies should not remain on the cross on the Sabbath (for that Sabbath was a high day), the Jews asked Pilate that their legs might be broken, and that they might be taken away. Then the soldiers came and broke the legs of the first and of the other who was crucified with Him. But when they came to Jesus and saw that He was already dead, they did not break His legs. But one of the soldiers pierced His side with a spear, and immediately blood and water came out. And he who has seen has* *testified, and his testimony is true; and he knows that he is telling the truth, so that you may believe"* (John 19:30-35).

The final hours of Jesus' life were like a clock ticking down. Time was running out, and Jerusalem was getting anxious. The greatest holiday in the Jewish calendar would begin in just three hours, and no one wanted to miss it. John 19:31 calls it Preparation Day, the day all Jews and all of Jerusalem prepared for, the most holy Sabbath of the year.

The Law was clear: no body could remain on a cross, no burial services held, no work performed on Preparation Day. The events at the cross must be done in three hours, or those involved would be unclean and unable to celebrate the feast. Everyone wanted to move on; it was time for Jesus to die.

RUSHING PAST THE TRUTH

In that three-hour span, the lamb needed to be killed and the house and children scrubbed. The meal had to be cooked. Friends gathered so they could be in place in case this was the year Messiah came.

You have to see the irony in all of this: The Lamb

of God is right before them, and they want to leave Him to prepare a dinner in His honor. Psychologists call this "change blindness." It describes how we miss something that is right before us because we get too accustomed to what we see. When something new comes, we cannot see it.

Jesus just called it blindness—having eyes but not seeing. The simple fact is that most of the people failed to see this Jesus dying on the cross as the promised, sacrificial Lamb bearing their sins once and for all.

The clock was ticking. No more than two hours were left now. The shadows were growing long, and the people were restless.

But before the end, Jesus gave us two last statements. They are among the most important words ever spoken, so we need to look at them closely. They were spoken for us. Everything Jesus did was on purpose and for our good. Before He died, He wanted to tie up the loose ends of our faith so we can enter joyfully into the greatness of the Resurrection. His words help us let go and move forward to the next stage of His plan for us.

Jesus spoke His final two statements in quick succession. The first of the two is perhaps the best known: "It is finished!" Some think they were Jesus' last words, but most scholars believe they were second to last. Undoubtedly, they are among the most important words Jesus ever spoke. They sealed our salvation.

From noon to 3 o'clock, great darkness covered on the earth. Yet Jesus said nothing. The people just waited and watched. After three hours of darkness, Jesus pushed himself up so He could speak and said, "It is finished!" He spoke clearly so everyone could hear Him.

The irony is that the people heard these words, but most misunderstood what Jesus was saying. Everyone knew He was dying, so they were not surprised to hear Him say what sounded like "I'm done. It's over." But Jesus' message was very different from what the crowd thought He was saying.

CRY OF VICTORY

If you don't understand why Jesus said these words, you will miss the power and good news they convey.

In the Greek, Jesus said just one word: *Tetelestai!*

It takes three English words to convey the idea, but they still don't adequately express the full power and action of what Jesus was saying to the world.

He wasn't admitting defeat. He had won and He knew it. *Teleo* means "to complete," signifying the successful end to a particular course of action. Jesus was saying, "I have completed my assignment; I have brought to a successful end that which I set out to do. The work is complete, with nothing left out or unfinished. I won! I have finished the task and defeated the enemy."

Tetelestai is the word you would use when you have climbed to the top of Mount Everest and look down at the earth or when you have completed your first marathon: "I did it!"

It's a word of victory. It doesn't mean "I survived" or "I made it." It means "I won. I did exactly what I set out to do, and I claim the champion's prize."

Imagine what the people thought beneath the cross that day. Is He crazy? He can't even understand that He's dying. He has lost!

That is what people think when they can't see clearly who Jesus is and what He is doing. They think

Christianity is for losers, when in reality it is all about victory. It's not just about suffering; it's about completion, success, and victory! A prevailing mood of Christianity should be triumph. The cross wins; Jesus' death defeats Satan.

But, we do not win the way the world wins. We win by giving our lives, by serving and not ruling. We win by giving, not taking.

"You know that the rulers of the Gentiles lord it over them, and those who are great exercise authority over them. Yet it shall not be so among you; but whoever desires to become great among you, let him be your servant. And whoever desires to be first among you, let him be your slave—just as the Son of Man did not come to be served, but to serve, and to give His life a ransom for many" (Matthew 20:25-28).

Don't get this wrong. As followers of Christ, we are not called to be complacent and to keep our talents under wraps so we can be humble. No, we give our best, do our best, and achieve our best. We face challenges and we overcome.

Christ conquered sin and all the forces of the world, not with an army but with His sacrifice. He gave His life. Satan will never serve anyone but himself. He will never give his life for anyone. But, in pride, he is defeated.

The cross of Jesus had purpose. On the cross, at the end of that horrible week, Jesus declares, "It's done! I've won!" That is why we as Christians can see the cross as our symbol of victory. We can embrace both its sorrow and its joy.

CRY OF COMPLETION

Second, "It is finished" declares that Jesus' mission was complete. It never has to be repeated. Jesus was saying, "This is the last time a sacrifice has to be made to pay for mankind's sins. It is enough. Once and for all."

"But Christ came as High Priest of the good things to come, with the greater and more perfect tabernacle not made with hands, that is, not of this creation. Not with the blood of goats and calves, but with His own blood He entered the Most Holy Place once for all, having obtained eternal redemption" (Hebrews 9:11, 12).

It is finished. *Tetelestai* is in the perfect tense,

meaning the victory of the cross continues. It is an action completed in the past with results continuing in the present. The impact of the work is as strong today as it was 2,000 years ago. The past tense says, "This happened!" But Jesus' statement said, "This happened and is still in effect today."

CRY OF PROPHECY

Third, Jesus was saying that there is more to come. He did not say, "*I* am finished." He said, "*It* is finished." There is a great difference.

"I am finished" could imply defeat or that Jesus had come up short. "It is finished" does not mean that Jesus is done or that His time is over. Jesus was not finished. The greatest ministry, success, and joy are still ahead of Him. He rose from the grave, and He ever lives to make intercession for us. He will come back and restore all things, and we will rule with Him forever. He is not finished. He has just begun.

God is not trying to sell you salvation. He's not offering salvation at half-price. He's not offering to go "dutch treat" with you. He's not offering salvation on an installment plan.

Jesus has finished His great task, but He isn't done. A new clock starts ticking. He is just moving on to the greater work as King of kings. He is the Grave Conqueror, Hell Destroyer, and Life Giver.

The cross is not the end. When Jesus died, the clock started to tick again—counting down to the Resurrection. There was more for Jesus after the cross and there is for us too. Resurrection!

We can miss this message if we get tunnel vision at Calvary. The cross is wonderful, but it is not a plaque that we put over a good man: "Here rests a good man. May his life be an example to us. Rest in peace." We must spend time at the cross to grasp the greatness of God's love and the enormity of our salvation. But Jesus' story doesn't end at the cross, and neither does ours.

Tony Campolo tells the story of when he was sixteen years old and his African-American friend Clarence died. Campolo went to the funeral—a funeral unlike any he had ever attended. The pastor preached from John 14:1: "Let not your heart be troubled. You believe in God, believe also in Me."

"Clarence has gone to heavenly mansions," the

pastor said. Then for the last twenty minutes of the sermon, he actually preached to the open casket. He yelled at the corpse. "Clarence! Clarence!" He spoke with such authority that Tony Campolo says he would not have been surprised had there been an answer.

"Clarence," the pastor said, "there were a lot of things we should have said to you that we never said. You got away too fast, Clarence. You got away too fast."

The pastor presented a litany of beautiful things that Clarence had done for people. When he finished, he said, "That's it, Clarence. There is nothing more to say when there is nothing more to say. There's only one thing to say. Good night, Clarence!"

And he grabbed the lid of the casket and slammed it shut.

Shockwaves went over the congregation.

Then the preacher lifted his face toward the ceiling and with a big smile on his face said, "Good night, Clarence! Good night, Clarence! Because I know that God is going to give you a good morning!"

The choir stood and started singing, "On that great

morning, we shall rise, we shall rise!" Soon people were dancing in the aisles and hugging each other.

Campolo said, "I knew the joy of the Lord, a joy that, in the face of death, laughs and sings, for there is no sting to death."

The clock of our sorrow is coming to an end, and a good day is ahead. The clock is ticking, and what is coming will be worth waiting for.

We are like the child waiting for Christmas or a birthday party. The clock seems to move so slowly. But the moment will come when joy breaks forth—a time to celebrate and receive eternal life. All of us who have received Him will share in His proclamation of victory: "It is finished!"

There is good news today. Jesus lived the perfect life, taught the perfect truth, and died the most horrible death. He did all this so that we could go forward in victory in this life and inherit new life beyond our comprehension.

What is your sin? If you confess it to Jesus and receive Him, then you can say as He did: "It's paid in full! It is finished!" You can move forward to fulfillment and joy and purpose.

Finishing is never as easy as it appears. The wedding ceremony was easy, but thirty-five years of marriage—now that has presented challenges I'm sure Andrea didn't anticipate. God's great plan for us includes times when we want to quit and give up.

Jesus gives us this encouragement from the Cross: You can do it and the result is going to be worth it. Just because life is hard and others think you're failing doesn't mean you are. Remember, you don't have to do everything perfectly. You simply need to do what God has assigned to you.

Hold on to God. He knows everything you're going through and has the power to see you safely to the other side. Remember, this trial doesn't have to be the end of your story. Your journey won't end in darkness and defeat, but rather at the throne of Jesus where you will rule with Him forever. Pray that God will give you strength for today and let the promise of a greater tomorrow fill your heart. You are not losing...wait and see.

People think Christianity is for losers, when in reality it is all about victory. It's not just about suffering; it's about completion, success and victory!

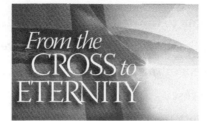

From the **CROSS** *to* **ETERNITY**

FATHER, INTO YOUR HANDS I COMMIT MY SPIRIT

"NOW IT WAS ABOUT THE SIXTH HOUR, *and there was darkness over all the earth until the ninth hour. Then the sun was darkened, and the veil of the temple was torn in two. And when Jesus had cried out with a loud voice, He said, 'Father, "into Your hands I commit My spirit."' Having said this, He breathed His last. So when the centurion saw what had happened, he glorified God, saying, 'Certainly this was a righteous Man!"'* (Luke 23:44-47).

So we come to the end: Jesus' last words, and then the tomb. What last words would you leave the world to help and encourage loved ones? Jesus left us words of trust and rest.

He also left us words of victory. He did not go out quietly; He shouted His final words because He wanted us to hear the end of His story and take the strength of those words to heart.

Every word Jesus spoke from the cross was for our benefit. Each statement had a purpose. And in this final statement, Jesus told us something important again. Each part of His last cry from the cross conveys promise, both for this life and the life to come.

RESTORED TO HIS FATHER

Let's examine each word He spoke:

"Father": The Father and Son relationship has been restored. The darkness of His soul has passed, sin has been paid for, and the smile of the Father is again on the Son. Jesus does not go out alone.

His first words on the cross were, "Father, forgive them." Then there was that terrible time when Jesus became sin and the Father looked away. At that point Jesus said, "My God, My God, why have You forsaken Me?" But finally He spoke to God as Father again, and He wanted the world to know the team is back. The burden has passed. He saw the Father's face and He wants us to know that sin has been defeated and all things are right.

"Into your hands": Jesus' eyes are on the Father's hands. For fifteen hours Jesus was in the hands of wicked men. With their hands they beat Him and slapped Him. They abused Him and hid their faces from Him. They put the crown of thorns on His head and ripped out His beard. They nailed Him to the cross. But through it all, neither their hands nor their hatred ever touched His soul.

For fifteen hours the hands of sinful man did what they wanted, but their time was at an end. Jesus saw the finish line, and His Father was there waiting with open hands.

The hands of a father are meant to be a wonderful place. The Father's hands are strong. They protect and they love; they approve and they bless. They hold on to you.

Jesus was not afraid of the Heavenly Father, and if

you are in Christ neither should you be. You are safe in the hands of the strong One who loves you the best.

Imagine the Heavenly Father smiling as He looks down from the edge of heaven. With a big smile He opens His arms and says, "Welcome home, Son."

"It's so good to be back, Father."

"I'm so proud of You, Son."

"Thank you, Father."

"I commit": *Commit* means to deposit something valuable in a safe and secure place. It's what you do when you take your will and your most valuable possessions and put them in a safe-deposit box at the bank.

"My spirit": Jesus referred to His life, His very existence. More than His physical body, He meant the real inner Him—the part that is most important.

So, in His final words, Jesus expressed complete faith in His Father. "Father, I have gone as far as I can go. I trust You and I rest in You. I put My life, My work, My journey into Your hands because I know everything is safe there. I know You will take it from here."

No one took Jesus' life; He gave it willingly. He

died in complete control, knowing what He had accomplished and where He was going.

"Therefore My Father loves Me, because I lay down My life that I may take it again. No one takes it from Me, but I lay it down of Myself. I have power to lay it down, and I have power to take it again. This command I have received from My Father" (John 10:17, 18).

REDISCOVERING OUR FATHER

What do Jesus' last words mean for us? They invite us to discover the unlimited trust our Heavenly Father deserves. There comes a time when we have to trust God and let go.

Each of us comes to that point when we reach the end of our ability. There are places we can't go and things we can't control. But we don't need to be in control.

Jesus' final statement is simple in its focus. He reminds us that life always comes down to the simplest thing—whom will we trust? To whom will we genuinely open ourselves?

No one can control life. There comes a point in

time when you have to find a place of release and rest. Jesus reminds us there is only one ultimate place anyone can be secure and truly rest: in the hands of the Heavenly Father.

But this simple truth runs counter to our natural instincts. We want to trust a person or organization or government agency or army or bank. We want to invest our lives in something tangible, believing that because of those resources everything is going to be all right. We can let go of the goals, the burdens, the fears, the hopes, the strategies, and the dreams. We can finally rest.

Our generation is searching for trust and rest. We imagine ourselves in control, yet what we long for is someone, something to trust completely. We fear a chaotic world out of control. Alone and vulnerable, we become weary and crave rest even more.

Sometimes it seems as if the world is falling in on us. We can't find a place to let go of the pressure. We cannot finish life on our own. In order to live up to life's demands and truly be all that we can be, we have to give ourselves to Someone stronger.

From the cross, Jesus calls to us to give our

burdens to the Father. His message is the same as it was throughout His life: "Come to Me, all you who labor and are heavy laden, and I will give you rest. Take My yoke upon you and learn from Me, for I am gentle and lowly in heart, and you will find rest for your souls" (Matthew 11:28, 29).

CHILDHOOD PRAYER, CHILDLIKE FAITH

Jesus' final words are a direct quotation from Scripture:

"For You are my rock and my fortress; therefore, for Your name's sake, lead me and guide me. Pull me out of the net which they have secretly laid for me, for You are my strength. *Into Your hand I commit my spirit*" (Psalm 31:3-5).

This passage is considered to be probably the first Scripture most Jewish children learned. Their mothers recited it every night at bedtime. So on the cross, as His life drained away, Jesus reverted to the prayer of His childhood, the prayer Mary taught him in Nazareth: "You are My rock and My strength. Into Your hand I commit My spirit...and I rest."

Something wonderful was happening. The human part of Jesus was great enough to be a child in the Father's hands.

Jesus didn't whisper His final prayer; He shouted it! "I'm going to rest now in the Father! The clock is set, and when it goes off you're going to see that I've won!"

Jesus didn't shout for the Father to hear; He shouted so you and I could hear. *It is finished, but this is not the end. Start the countdown. Satan is defeated. Hell is going to crumble. The grave will not hold Me. I'm coming back.*

Three simple life applications echo through our lives when we respond to Jesus' last words.

1: Do the Right Thing and Leave the Results to God

The best way to get through life is to stop trying to control results or people and just do the right thing, knowing that God brings the ultimate results. You can't control results; that's God's business. Your responsibility is to do the right thing, the honorable thing, and let God take care of the rest.

I learned years ago that I can't control the world. I can't control people or even my own life. But as I rely on God, I can always try to do the right thing.

When you focus on controlling your circumstances, you usually miss the best that God can do in and through you. I live by what I call Ross' Law of Leadership—"What you control, you lose. But what you give to others can remain forever."

Leaders don't try to control; they lead. Trying to control people is like herding cats. You can't drive them, but you can lead them with love and security and they will choose to follow.

A great business leader was once asked, "What is your secret?" The reply: "I don't control people. I just give the right vision, opportunity, and support, and God takes care of the rest."

One of the most important lessons you can learn is to separate yourself and your worth from short-term goals and success. Simply sow the right seed. God brings the harvest in His time, and His harvest is multiplied.

Success is not how much you have; it's how faithful you are. It involves following God both when it's easy and when it's hard. Do the right thing and let God take care of everything else.

Sometimes we think we can't do all that needs to be done. We don't have to do it all; we just need to do our best. When the challenges of life are overwhelming and the tasks look impossible, we do what is possible and let God work His supernatural plan.

God created life so that we cannot live it well without His blessing. We weren't designed to carry the weight of the world and take care of every little thing along the way. We were created to live in His power and His blessing as we operate in His strength and express His love.

2: Beginning Is Good, but Finishing Is Better

You have to begin the journey if you want to win. The old proverb, "The journey of a thousand miles begins with the first step," holds true. Without that step, you can never reach your destination. There can be no victory, no transformed life, no success unless you begin.

God doesn't explain everything about the road

ahead or how to accomplish the work. He just calls you to begin and follow Him in both good times and hard times.

Victory and reward is in store for those who finish their race. Jesus tells us this from the cross, and the apostle Paul echoes it this way:

"I have fought the good fight, I have finished the race, I have kept the faith. Finally, there is laid up for me the crown of righteousness, which the Lord, the righteous Judge, will give to me on that Day, and not to me only but also to all who have loved His appearing" (2 Timothy 4:7, 8).

You can't run the whole race today, but you can take a step. We overestimate what we can do in the short haul, but underestimate what we can do over time. The goal is simply to keep at it, recognizing that God is working through us in His time according to His plan.

Find something you can do and do it. Then find another thing and do it. Work the list, and watch as God works His promises. Remember, God's reward awaits after you have done His will. The crown is at the finish line, not after the first lap.

Some assignments we finish regularly: Painting a picture. Finishing the sermon. Cutting the lawn. Cleaning the basement.

Other assignments we will never finish. We carry the baton until Jesus tells us to pass it along to another. Until then, we run, even if we run a little slower. I finished high school, but I never finish learning. I finished raising my children, but I'll never finish encouraging and guiding them. I finished a sermon, but I'm working on another one.

We have to keep running the race. Beginning is good, but God has called us to finish. So we go forward, taking the next step in God's great plan.

3: God Is Your Father

It is a life-transforming moment when you discover the power of spiritual rest. The key to that discovery is realizing that God is your Father.

People need someone in their life who is better and stronger than they are. That Person is God the Father. No matter how tough and talented you are, you were designed to be in relationship with Him. He is our Heavenly Father.

Jesus was saying: "Father, I've gone as far as I can and as far as I should. Now I leave it in Your hands. I rest in You."

Our relationship to the Heavenly Father is essential. We need Jesus, the Savior, and we need the Holy Spirit and His power. But we also need the Father's hands.

Each of us has a choice—we can keep trying to carry the burdens of life by ourselves, or we can put our lives in God's hands and say, "I trust You. I'm going to rest."

Jesus gives His spirit to the Father. The work is finished. The time of death is recorded. The people go home to get ready for the Sabbath. Jesus' friends place His body in a borrowed grave. The door is sealed.

And then the clock starts ticking.

Redemption has been purchased. No other sacrifice for sin remains, and now the clock starts counting to victory. Two days...one day...10 hours...one hour...10 minutes...9...8...7...6...Resurrection!

Jesus wants us to understand the cross, because it is the foundation of our salvation. But the cross is not the end. Jesus said, "Don't forget what I have done, but don't stop here. Something great is going to happen. Resurrection is coming. My resurrection guarantees your own."

Jesus paid for our sins, and He wants us to live in the power of His resurrection. Every week I go back to the cross to make sure I have everything in the right place and established on the right foundation. Then I ask God to empower me with resurrection life to move forward.

Because of the cross, we can say, "It is finished," even as we acknowledge that Jesus is still working and the best is ahead.

I like how an old Nigerian hymn expresses it:

> Nothing either great or small,
> Nothing, sinner, no,
> Jesus did it, did it all,
> Long, long ago.

> "It is finished!" Yes, indeed,
> Finished every jot:
> Sinner, this is all you need,
> Tell me is it not?

When He, from His lofty throne,
Stooped to do and die,
Everything was fully done:
Hearken to His cry.

Weary, working, burdened one,
Wherefore toil you so?
Cease your doing; all was done,
Long, long ago.

Till to Jesus' work you cling
By a simple faith,
"Doing" is a deadly thing,
"Doing" leads to death.

Cast your deadly "doing" down,
Down at Jesus' feet:
Stand in Him, in Him alone,
Gloriously complete.

Surrendering control is not as easy as it sounds. Yet at some point in life we all realize that much of life is beyond our control. We aren't powerful enough or smart enough to know what to do.

The good news is that our Heavenly Father is

both wise and powerful. We can trust Him to work all things together for good. The longer I serve Jesus, the more I discover that I don't want to control life or other people. When I surrender control of the consequences to God, I am blessed. I find rest from my labor and acquire an expectation that God will do above and beyond what I thought possible.

Today, go as far as God reveals the way to you. Then give the rest to Him. Surrender your life to Him anew with this triumphant prayer: Father, I have gone as far as I can go. Now I ask You to take this situation all the way to victory.

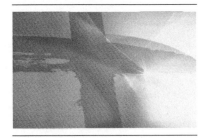

*Jesus reminds us
there is only one ultimate
place anyone can be
secure and truly rest:
in the hands of
the Heavenly Father.*

CHAPTER EIGHT

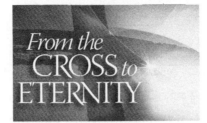

LIFE'S GREATEST DECISION

by Randy Hurst

TWO GREAT MOMENTS

Two great moments in our lives are when we are born and when we discover why we were born. We were created for a reason—a divine purpose. Our lives are not accidents or fate. They did not happen by chance. God was working in our lives even before we were born. He loves us, and He has a personal plan for each of us. His purpose in our lives can only be accomplished because of Jesus Christ.

TWO GREAT QUESTIONS

To understand and live God's purpose, we must

know the answers to two questions about Jesus. Who was He? Why did He give His life?

1. *Who was Jesus Christ?* The life of Jesus Christ is the turning point of all history. He was a man from the small town of Nazareth in Palestine, a carpenter's son. Many in the world admire and respect Him and believe that He was a great teacher and even a prophet. But He was much more. He was God the Son in human form—the promised Savior. The Bible says, "There is one God and one Mediator between God and men, the Man Christ Jesus" (1 Timothy 2:5).

2. *Why did Jesus give His life?* Jesus' life was not taken from Him. He gave it. Jesus said, "My Father loves Me, because I lay down My life that I may take it again. No one takes it from Me, but I lay it down of Myself. I have power to lay it down, and I have power to take it again" (John 10:17-18).

Jesus gave his life for two essential reasons. First, because we are sinners. Second, because we could do nothing about it.

We can't have God's plan happen in our lives when we are separated from Him. Our sin comes between us and God. It separates us from His plan for us. But, God made a way to forgive us, save us from everlasting punishment, and bring about His plan for our lives. He sent His Son, Jesus Christ, to pay the penalty for our sins.

Jesus was born as a man, but He lived His life without sinning. Men lied about Him and judged Him guilty of things He had never done. Then they hung Him on a cross to die. Although He never sinned, He was punished for sin. So death had no power over Him, and He came back to life after three days. Now He gives everlasting life to anyone who receives Him.

TWO ROADS

Jesus Christ taught that every person will exist for eternity. Life has only two roads, and we are each on one of them. One leads to death and eternal punishment—the other to everlasting life. The apostle Paul wrote to the Roman Christians: "For the wages of sin is death, but the gift of God is eternal life in Christ Jesus our Lord" (Romans 6:23). He also taught that being saved from sin's penalty is not easy—but it is simple: "If you confess with your mouth the Lord Jesus and believe in your heart that God has raised Him from the dead, you will be saved" (Romans 10:9).

Everyone knows there is a difference between right and wrong. Even if we have never read a Bible or do not understand what it means to sin against God, we can know we are sinners, because God created each of us with a conscience. We know what we don't want others to do to us. We don't want them to steal our possessions, lie about us or be unkind to us. When we do to someone what we don't want done to us, our conscience lets us know we have done wrong.

The penalty for sin is death. That is why all people die. But two thousand years ago, Jesus Christ, the holy Son of God, became a man. For thirty-three years He lived without sin. Then He was killed. He paid the penalty for sin without committing the crime. So death had no power over Him. After three days, He came back to life again. He is alive! And now He offers forgiveness of sin and the gift of everlasting life to everyone who will ask Him.

You can receive Christ as your Savior right now, this moment! You don't have to be in a church or special place, or have the help of a minister or priest.

You can pray now, wherever you are. God is listening. Tell Him in your own words that you are sorry for your sins and that you want to receive Jesus Christ as your Savior and Lord. Ask God to help you change your heart and life. It's your prayer He wants to hear.

If it will help, you can pray this prayer. But you can't just say the words. You must mean them from your heart:

"God, I know *I have sinned. I believe Your Son, Jesus Christ, died to take the punishment for my sin. I believe Jesus came back to life from death and has the power to forgive my sin and change my life. Please forgive me. Come into my life and change me. I want to live for You because you died for me. I want to follow Your plan for my life. I believe You have forgiven me, and I thank You for hearing my prayer, in Jesus' name."*

If you prayed and meant it from your heart, God has forgiven you. God knew before you were born that you would receive His Son as your Savior. Now you can begin the life He has planned for you! God will lead you step by step to what He has chosen for you. He will show you the way to live and will teach you each day, as you grow spiritually and become the person He planned for you to be.

Your decision to receive and follow Christ is not just a ritual or part of a religion. It is a relationship. These three things will greatly help you in your relationship with Jesus and help you to grow spiritually.

First—*You need spiritual food.* You know that if you don't eat for a few days your body gets weak. You are not just a body. Your spirit needs food like your body does, or you will become spiritually weak. The Bible is God's Word. It is like spiritual food. We suggest you start by spending just five or ten minutes each day reading the Bible. You can start with the Gospel of Mark, which is the earliest and shortest record of the life of Jesus.

Second—*You need to pray each day.* In any personal relationship, we need to talk to each other. When you read your Bible each day, spend time talking to God. Just speak to Him in your own words from your heart. Also spend a few moments just quietly thinking about what you've read in the Bible. God will communicate to your heart and guide you.

Third—*You need a spiritual family.* That's what a church is. We can't make it in life alone. A church family will help you grow stronger in Christ. They will be there to encourage you, be your friends and pray with you. So, find a church home and be there every Sunday. Attend a church where Christ is honored, the Bible is taught and everyone is welcome.

Receiving Christ opens the way for God's plan and purpose for your life. It is truly life's greatest decision.